# WHAT I WISH
# I KNEW

## The Wisdom Gained From Relationships, Love, and Lust

*by*

JOSH POWELL

## WHAT I WISH I KNEW: THE WISDOM GAINED FROM RELATIONSHIPS, LOVE, AND LUST.

For permission requests, write to the publisher, addressed "Attention: Permissions Coordinator," 205 N. Michigan Avenue, Suite #810, Chicago, IL 60601. 13th & Joan books may be purchased for educational, business or sales promotional use. For information, please email the Sales Department at sales@13thandjoan.com.

Printed in the U. S. A.

First Printing, November 2023
Library of Congress Cataloging-in-Publication Data has been applied for.
ISBN: 978-1-961863-20-0

## Dedication

This book is dedicated to those passionate about the healing process, those who want to become the best version of themselves but question what the journey looks like. This book is dedicated to those looking to grow and find purposeful relationships that serve you and others well and align with where you want to go in life. The journey is about effort, not perfection.

# Contents

# Acknowledgments

Giving thanks and praise to Heavenly Father and Mother
for allowing me the opportunity to share. I'd like to
acknowledge those I've failed, the ones I've constantly let
down, and everyone I've hurt and disappointed. Please
know that I am a work in progress, working daily on
being a better me. My effort is genuine. I'm learning a
new me every day. This book is to express the importance
of the journey, the fight, and, most importantly, the fight
for self. I love and appreciate every person I've connected
with, whether family, friend, teammate, or businessperson.
I strive to be who the Creator destined me to be.

# A Letter to the Reader

I'M GLAD YOU'RE HERE AND incredibly thankful for your open mind and heart.

*What I Wish I Knew* was developed with great intention – to share pieces of my life story, experiences, and wisdom gained over the years to help us navigate healthier relationships with others and with self.

Striving to become healthier versions is not to be taken lightly. Growing in wisdom and self-awareness leads to attracting what serves us, including people, circumstances, and situations. Everything outside that attraction will fall by the wayside because we know and value our lives. We cannot help ourselves (or society) move forward and leave the past behind us if we stay stuck in unhealthy habits, mind frames, and patterns. We cannot have thriving, long-term relationships without self-awareness, reflection, and growth.

Doing better and being better— ultimately evolving as individuals, leads to change, especially making wiser, swifter, firmer decisions without diving down the rabbit hole of guilt, shame, confusion, and toxic pattern-repetitive behaviors. You see, healed people can still attract an unhealed or unhealthy situation because your heart could be so big that you want to see others feel better, too, or you haven't found and nurtured your inner voice to make better decisions for yourself. Through *What I Wish I Knew*, shared experiences are not meant to encourage a trauma bond but to encourage you to acknowledge your areas of growth to overcome, love yourself without remaining in a broken place, and pinpoint ways to elevate relationships. Everyone experiences pain or brokenness, but let us focus on the solution.

# Introduction

VERY OFTEN, WITHOUT REALIZING IT, people involved in toxic relationships repeat negative patterns from their childhood. When engaged in unhealthy situations, people are likely to avoid forming genuine, close relationships, or they opt to keep partners at an emotional distance. They may hide their feelings, push people away, keep secrets, and lack real intimacy within their relationships. Despite those behaviors, most people in toxic relationships desire a genuine, safe connection yet feel alone when in relationships or pursuing them because they are uncomfortable giving and receiving healthy love. Not only that, but they may not know how to give and receive healthy love because it was never modeled or given to them. That mistrust can accustom people to rejection, lead others to emotionally close off or avoid, and feel uncomfortable showing affection. When hurt by the people who supposedly love and care for you, such as family, friends, partners, or other loved ones, it only makes sense why many grow up having a tough time loving themselves, trusting people, opening up to others, and forming lasting, healthy relationships. Healing is critical in leaving those behaviors and mind frames behind, but acknowledgment and self-awareness are necessary first steps to begin your self-improvement journey.

*  *  *

I was born in Charleston, South Carolina, the only child of my parents. At the age of two, my mom and dad divorced. According to my mom, there was heightened tension between them, so she made the difficult decision to leave. Although that was a significant transition in my life, I don't remember much of it, but I do recall my mom continually asking me how I was feeling. She tried her best to stay in tune with my feelings during this change.

Mom and I moved from Charleston to Atlanta, Georgia, where she did what was necessary to keep a roof over my head. That meant working several jobs, including a youth program role that didn't pay enough to cover the rent. She also worked as a dispatcher with the Fulton County Emergency Center and later applied to the Fulton County Sheriff's Department, where she earned a new position. I was still relatively young, and she hated the idea of leaving me at home alone during her 11-hour days, so she decided to let me live with my aunt and uncle in Toccoa, Georgia, about two hours away from Atlanta. Mom explained that life wasn't going for her as planned, none of which was my fault, and that I had to live elsewhere while she sorted things out. I listened and did what I was told. Whether it was reverence for my mom or just the natural ability of a child to do as told, I didn't question her, nor did I feel abandoned or confused. So, my aunt agreed to keep me for a while, but during my stay with them, my grandparents came to pick me up, deeming I was better off with them, and they never took me back. Everyone handles and processes change differently. Thankfully, I didn't see myself as lost in the shuffle, simply growing up with different family members at times.

For the next few years, while living with my grandparents, I learned structure and discipline. As much as children want to roam free and do as they please, they crave structure. Structure provides safety, emotionally and physically speaking. My grandparents were very traditional in terms of discipline. Respect was the standard. Saying "yes, ma'am" and "no, ma'am" was the norm, and I abided by their rules. They taught me morals and values that continue to guide my decisions today. Respect, hard work, and the importance of family were principles they preached. My grandparents also taught me the meaning of gratitude and appreciation, especially for things we may take for granted at an early age, such as food on the table and clothes on our backs. I listened to everything they told me without them having to repeat themselves—the respect factor was definitely present. My strong work ethic developed early in life by watching my grandparents work hard to care for me and each other. I would help them clean the sawdust mill and sell biscuits on the weekend, so I had firsthand work experience and a firm grasp on the importance of discipline in the real world.

"Keep God first," they often said, instilling a level of faith in me that I had not yet received.

During that time, my grandparents made sure to include faith in nearly every lesson. We attended every service and bible study consistently as they laid the foundation for me to nurture and develop my relationship with God.

"Honor your parents," they preached, and although I no longer lived with my mom, it was never lost on me to give my mother the utmost respect.

My grandmother was a graceful woman. I never heard her cuss; she was a peaceful soul but had no problem disciplining me when I got out of line. Through her firm but fair approach, I began understanding the duality of peace and structure – both were needed to maintain an emotionally healthy life.

My grandfather had a strong presence. He was a man of few words, but when he spoke, people listened. He was a military veteran and had every award you could think of, including the Purple Heart and the Congressional Medal of Honor. As a couple, he and my grandmother always seemed on the same page. They were the personification of the saying "equally yoked." I never saw them argue or disrespect one another. Maybe they fussed behind closed doors, I don't know, but I do know that they modeled a healthy relationship. They communicated respectfully and made decisions together. They had a solid understanding of one another, which gave me a sense that they were a solid couple. I watched the example they set for our family; from my standpoint, they were the epitome of true love. It's a wonder why those principles didn't carry over into the lives of others in our family. As an adult, I understand that you can lead a horse to water but can't make it drink.

I remember the day my mom came back for me. It was very unexpected. I was surprised to see her yet happy because I missed my mom so much. I was around nine years old, and I quickly learned she had a fiancé and he had two older sons. This news was a massive adjustment because I went from being an only child to having two older stepbrothers overnight. The peace I felt at my grandparents' house was replaced with chaos under my mom's roof with my new siblings. For some reason, it seemed like we could never quite get along. Was it because I was the youngest? I'm not sure, but we bumped heads often, and I always felt like they messed with me beyond the torment a younger sibling is expected to endure. They had no boundaries. There were times when our parents weren't home, and my brothers took full advantage of that by throwing parties. Sometimes, my stepbrothers would threaten me to make sure I wouldn't say anything about what they were doing. They would bring girls over to have sex and had the audacity to use my bed. At nine, I was well aware of sex because I saw it, heard it, and smelled it, which led me to put two and two together about what was going down.

As the little brother, I didn't want to be alienated from them. So, I never said a word. Eventually, I began isolating myself from everyone, leading to other changes. Self-isolation led to the point where I wasn't saying much at all. Soon after that, my attitude became a problem. I became short with my mother and standoffish. I didn't communicate as much as before, which wasn't like me because I always had an open door to her. My mother noticed this and decided I needed to see a therapist. She could sense that I was overwhelmed by my new surroundings and knew that action was needed, yet she didn't know the issues that had taken place since my stepbrothers entered the picture. Although I was overwhelmed by my new life, I was also treated poorly and constantly witnessed dysfunction.

One night, home life became too intense. My brother had been talking recklessly, threatening me, and warning me about "what I better not do."

"I never liked you," he reminded me.

"You always seem to get what you want," he stated.

"You better not say anything or bring up anything old," he threatened, "or I'll beat you up."

What happened next was a blur. The threats became too much. I wanted my peace back, the same peace I had with my grandparents. I wanted to be left alone once and for all. So, I went into my mother's closet, the place I watched her store her weapon, the same weapon she told me never to touch. I quickly grabbed her gun, put it to my brother's head, and pulled the trigger. I remember it like it was yesterday. He was playing video games but suddenly dropped the controller. Fear and shock took over as he lost control of his video game, then yelled for my mother and stepfather. The next thing I remember, Mom was furious about the incident.

"I told you never to touch that gun," she yelled. "You could get a lot of people hurt. I could go to jail!" she screamed.

We dodged a bullet that night, literally and figuratively, because the gun was not fully loaded. In a split second, my life could have drastically changed. Soon after that, I found myself getting into fights at school, and I was jumped a few times in the neighborhood, whether I deserved it or not. Things seemed to spiral out of control until I found the sport I fell in love with – basketball. The moment I watched my mom play in a local rec basketball league was the moment an Atlanta-based football coach approached me and said I needed to be on the basketball court. Basketball was like that first crush you fall in love with and never seem to forget. Playing basketball gave me something to look forward to despite what I endured at home and school. For the first time in quite some time, I felt a sense of belonging and family.

As I got older, my dad and I would spend Christmas and summers together. Throughout my childhood, he was in and out of jail, mainly for child support issues, but I remember the holidays together vividly. I thoroughly enjoyed time with my old man. Whenever I would visit him, the first thing we would do was go to the mall and shop. I would get any and everything I wanted. That was how we started every trip. I liked it when we would drive around Charleston, and he would work on cars. I just loved being in his presence. At the time, my old man could do no wrong in my eyes. The little moments always stood out, which made my dad seem larger than life. Memories of picking out any snack I wanted from the gas station and teaching me about mechanics remain fresh in my mind. As we grow, we realize the little things are never really little.

My dad eventually remarried, and just like my mother's new marriage, I had to learn to adjust to a new family dynamic. Apparently, my dad had other children I never knew existed. I had an older brother and two older sisters. Around ten years old, I finally met them for the first time.

My siblings and I were often alone in my dad's house while he and his wife worked during the day. So, entertaining each other became familiar territory. Family members would come over and stay with us, and we would talk about everything, mostly music, sex, and who was crushing on who. During one of our many conversations, I remember an older family member telling me I wasn't blood-related to them. That statement was followed by questions like "Do you like me?" and "Do you think I'm cute?" Then, the questions shifted to conversations like "Let me show you something." Those conversations eventually led to my first sexual experience, which started as "closet play." The touching and feeling were a subtle invitation to sexual intercourse. I was oblivious to the fact that I was being groomed and abused. As a child, I did not recognize this behavior as sexual abuse, but we would have sex or do sexual things often. It seemed normal at the time because I thought everyone was doing it, so it never crossed my mind that any of it was wrong.

The dysfunction of my parents' respective households made me feel like this was a way of life. Later in life, I realized how those experiences shaped my future. This trauma set the course for a pattern of behaviors that caused me to function a certain way in relationships throughout my young life, including an inability and unwillingness to commit, a difficult time trusting my partners and expressing my feelings, and constant worry about whether they liked me for me.

Over time, family sexual escapades stopped. My spirit wasn't right, but I also began dealing with older women. Pandora's box had been opened, and my appetite for the next sexual experience outweighed my prior experiences. I had been over-sexualized, which affected my interpersonal relationships as a teenager. I was either in a relationship or dealing with a young lady, but I wanted to be involved with other girls, too. As the effects of my abuse lingered, I constantly had sex with other females, mainly older women. There was a lack of commitment because my sexual appetite was my only focus. In a nutshell, sports, the opposite sex, and sex were my life. I experienced constant sexual urges, and the effects of mental, physical, and emotional abuse remained alive. I was all over the place.

During my junior year in high school, I began playing AAU basketball. The weekends were crazy— crazy as in something a young man should never experience. My OG, one of the guys who ran the team, would tell my mom where to drop me off unless he picked me up from our house, and he would take my teammates and me to the mall and buy us everything we needed – clothes, shoes, you name it. We didn't have to pack a bag because he would get everything we needed with him. Stepping out at night after practice or a game was our routine. Our first stop was always the nightclub. Then, we would go to a strip club. I was a teenager, years from the legal drinking age, sleeping with 30-plus-year-old women. The things I heard, saw, and experienced at that age still blow my mind to this day – going to clubs, sleeping with older women, fighting, learning how to talk to older women, being in the streets, witnessing violence, watching thousands get thrown at the strip club, hanging out with entertainers and street dudes, and sleeping for a mere four hours from Friday to Sunday.

When thinking back on that time in my life, I realize the distinct difference between my 15-year-old self and the man I am today. Today, I enjoy real connections, long walks, and good meals. I appreciate depth. I understand the power of saying no. I no longer have to drink, do drugs, or sleep with women to enjoy myself. My connection with God is stronger than before, which guides me. I read and write as forms of enjoyment. I welcome opportunities to be a better me. The man I am today is night and day to the young man I was at 15. Nevertheless, I am grateful for everything I experienced because those situations molded me into this version of myself. With all the unhealthy experiences and early exposure, a simpler life has become my preference.

That same year, at 16 years old, I remember my stepfather being upset with me because he felt I didn't include him in my college decision. We were not close, although I did respect him as a father figure. Understandably, he was upset because he felt left out of the decision-making process. However, we lacked closeness. The support was there, but the bond was not. Anyway, I was sitting at the kitchen table, eating a bowl of oatmeal for dinner after practice, when he came behind me and smacked me on the back of my head with his belt, which caused my face to go into my bowl of hot oatmeal. At that moment, I wanted to kill him, but I got up, wiped my face, and listened to what he had to say, remembering my grandparents' lectures about respecting adults. After he spoke, I walked into my mother's room and told her I could no longer stay at her home. I expressed to her that staying in her home wouldn't lead to a good outcome, mainly because the way he spoke to me and treated her at times was unbearable. She was devastated, but she understood.

My mother thought I went to live with close family friends, but I went back and forth to friends' houses, sometimes sleeping in cars. I was practically homeless until I moved in with a friend. But the thing is, she was more than a friend; she was someone I was intimate with and had feelings for, so this wasn't a platonic living situation. Her mother, whom I grew close with, allowed me to sleep on the couch during most of my senior year, not knowing that her daughter and I were more than friends. When she found out, though, she asked us to respect the rules of her home, as she did not condone our behavior. As defiant teens, we listened to an extent, but we were still intimate from time to time.

Nevertheless, I learned how to mask what I was going through by keeping my grades up and staying out of trouble. Through all of that turmoil, I graduated with honors, ranked 26th in my class with a 3.7 GPA, and was a member of the Beta Club, an honors organization that recognizes outstanding academic achievement, promotes strong moral character and social responsibility, encourages service to others, fosters leadership skills, and provides the setting for students to develop strong interpersonal skills. (I have to give myself some flowers.)

I had five schools in mind regarding the next step of my basketball career – the University of North Carolina, North Carolina State University, the University of Florida, Georgia Tech, and the University of Georgia. I chose North Carolina State because the current players who played my position were graduating, which gave me a chance to shine in that role and get away from home, too. Not only that but when Coach Bobby Cremins retired and UGA got in trouble for allegedly giving money to their players, my choices narrowed down. When I went on my official visit to NC State, I fell in love with the school and didn't need to look any further. The energy of the campus felt great; it felt like home, and I knew I would receive a good education, so all the dots seemed to connect for me. Lastly, NC State was close enough for me to visit home but far enough away to experience independence.

After only two years, I decided to leave college to pursue my professional dream and financially help my mother. Although she never asked for financial help, she was candid about letting me know about her struggles, so I lent a hand. I had a long career in the NBA and overseas, playing for esteemed organizations such as the Dallas Mavericks, Atlanta Hawks, Houston Rockets, and Los Angeles Lakers and in countries such as China, Italy, Australia, and Greece, among others.

Living in foreign countries, working with several different coaches, and playing alongside countless other athletes paved the way for life lessons I'll have forever. Needless to say, I learned a lot on and off the court. Basketball helped me grow as a man, develop better habits, and become culturally aware, all of which added to the values and principles I learned from childhood. Traveling and being a part of different teams was humbling, especially when learning other languages and experiencing new customs, cultures, and traditions. Importantly, I learned about financial stability, relationships, and what successful relationships entail. Twenty years of playing professionally required discipline and hard work, and I held steady in those areas.

Over the years, I've had several relationships and entered into marriages. My first marriage ended in divorce after ten years. I grew from that marriage, and although it didn't end the way we planned, I took the lessons to future relationships—I learned to forgive myself for my shortcomings and show grace to my partner for hers, too; be a better communicator; have patience and more understanding, take accountability, and avoid making excuses. Through this level of knowledge, I learned to love myself better and to love others better, too.

As someone who experienced sexual abuse, relationships are viewed differently, and sex does not have the same meaning as it would to someone without those experiences. At one point, I viewed relationships as a physical exchange, believing people connected for surface-level reasons. Sex was a means of connection without vulnerability — you just do it to do it, but avoiding creating a bond wasn't healthy. Regardless of how things worked out in past relationships, I am beyond blessed to be a father to my beautiful children.

I merely scratched the surface of my life by sharing those moments, but my vision is intentional. By sharing personal trials, tribulations, lessons, and wisdom, I hope to help others communicate effectively, recognize and overcome toxic behaviors, remove excuses, and do what it takes to have healthy, meaningful relationships, relationships that not only last and thrive but deepen within and between two people who are intentional about growing together. Life is meant to be shared, especially its lessons, and although people must experience life for themselves to grow, there is much to learn from those who have been there and done that. With gratitude and humility, may my successes, failures, shortcomings, and strengths help you on your unique journey.

## Chapter One

# ROLE MODELS

*"He who wants good, let him first be good."*

Johann Wolfgang von Goethe

M ANY HAVE ROLE MODELS, WHETHER their parents, siblings, athletes, public figures, or musicians. Everyone looks up to someone. A role model serves as an example of the morals, thoughts, and behaviors associated with a role. Role models, however, can be positive and negative influences. When we recognize someone as a role model, we tend to focus on their achievements, qualities, and the example they set. In many cases, mainly those who follow their role models closely, those examples are what we use to pattern our lives as adults.

My grandparents were major inspirations in my life. My grandmother, Precious, a heavy churchgoer and believer who loved God, was a moral role model. My grandfather, Pampa, who loved going on drives where we cleaned up the roads, was a living, breathing example of an honorable man. During those times together, he would talk to me about life, and I absorbed those conversations like a sponge. Precious was the type of person that would tell me to love and pray for anyone that wronged her. She explained that God wants us to live with a forgiving, gracious spirit. Precious and Pampa weren't rockstars, professional athletes, or famous entertainers, but they were my role models that modeled honesty and love in their purest forms. I am thankful for their wisdom, guidance, and how they molded me to think differently. However, I shied away from those lessons when surrounded by other adults who were role models in my life, too, just not in the same moral fashion.

Childhood experiences teach us and mold us. Your experiences profoundly affect your relationships, and my experiences were no different. Although I had incredible examples of role models from my grandparents, my childhood trauma ultimately shaped how I interacted in adult relationships. My trauma molded my view of relationships and how I was supposed to function in them. For example, growing up, the people that hurt me most were those with the most access to me, which included family and friends. So, it was no surprise that I expected to experience hurt as an adult. On the other end, trauma makes it hard to be fully present for yourself and others, and you may have your guard up because you're always looking for something as if relationships cannot be pure or honest. Thankfully, blessings are in the lessons.

Childhood trauma can affect us in many ways. The manifestation of unresolved childhood trauma can surface in our parenting skills and how we react to triggers and affect our relationships. The saying is true—hurt people, hurt people. If you don't do the work to heal or learn the lessons from your past, you will hurt yourself and everyone in your path.

As a present, active father, I realize I am also protective, wanting to shield my children from everything. That seems universal among parents. We have an innate feeling to shield our kids from harm and only expose them to what's good and pure. As a protective father, I mean well, but being overly guarded is not always the answer. Then again, this instinct has helped me bond and connect with my children even more. I am driven to educate them, teach them about life and relationships, and share advice about everything under the sun. The better equipped they are with knowledge, the better they will handle various situations life may throw their way. If I had been better emotionally equipped as a child, I could have navigated hardships with family and friends in a healthier manner. Although I was not equipped then, I am now in a position to guide my children by sharing the wisdom I've gained through experience and self-reflection, wisdom that sticks with me to this day:

1. Keep God first.
2. Be yourself.
3. Always do the right thing no matter who's watching.
4. Lead by example. Let your actions speak louder than your words, although both should match.
5. Prayer changes things. Drawing back to the first lesson, placing God first will lead to better outcomes. Better may not be what you want, but what He deems best is far more important.

Although I recognized my grandparents' greatness, I did not realize how quickly the core values instilled in me by them would be tested. I had to immediately put them into play once I started living with my mother, her husband, and his sons. Looking back, I think about how they mistreated me and how challenging it was to manage. Because of that experience, I recognize my difficulties in trusting others. Although dwelling in the past is not productive, reflection is valuable because it allows you to recognize your growth. Back then, I asked myself so many questions:

Why am I being treated this way?

Why am I being talked to like this?

Why am I being threatened at times?

Does everyone go through this?

These people say they love and care for me, so why should I love and pray for people who treat me this way?

I knew what my grandmother had taught me, but everyone has limits, right? If not for the foundation laid by my grandparents and the lessons they instilled from a young age, I would have struggled on a deeper level to make sense of those questions as an adult. Seeing and experiencing different examples of love and trust helped me sort through those emotions. Unpleasant experiences often lead to fruitful lessons and wisdom.

Receiving lessons as I continue to grow is a gift and a curse. I have often gone through life looking sideways at people and circumstances, always waiting for the bad to rear its ugly head. The more I mature, elevate, and become my best self, the more I invite positive energy into my life. I don't have to watch my back in the same manner because I'm not attracting negative energy. I know to remove myself if that energy presents itself, whether in another person, situation, or circumstance. This requires mindfulness and discipline, but the outcome is worth the journey. Most important is doing the inner work and living in a healthy space, regardless of the people around you. So, what does "doing the work" look like?

This differs for everyone.

In my life, doing the work means building and sustaining habits to form a healthier version of myself. Doing the work means reading, writing, and meditating. Doing the work means being still and present to maintain a clear mind. I also sought therapy to learn about myself and unpack the past to grow stronger for the future. Doing the work also means holding myself accountable for my actions and remaining responsible for my decisions. I am committed to building a better relationship with God and surrounding myself with the right people.

If you look at "doing the work" in an uplifting, life-changing way, your entire perspective of life will shift for the better. You will inevitably avoid growth and peace if you look at "doing the work" as a daunting, torturous process. The choice is yours. I decided to tackle my trauma head-on, which meant unpacking the effects of abuse. Looking back, I see how past trauma affected my relationships, and as I peel back the scabs of my trauma, I realize it was a two-fold situation. On one end, I learned and adapted to the dark side but also witnessed how people act and move within the confines of a relationship, whether romantically, platonically, or professionally. I studied many sides of people and learned how they treat others based on their true intentions, which may not be revealed immediately. Why do they stay engaged in these relationships? Through firsthand experience, I understand intent, learn about the face of manipulative behavior, and identify toxic traits while knowing what something good looks like. On the other end, I learned a lot from my past trauma because it helped me understand my likes and dislikes. I also better understand what's healthy for me regarding relationships with family, friends, and potential dating partners. Moving forward, I use the knowledge I've gained to develop meaningful relationships with value, relationships worth fighting for while continuing my growth as a man.

Because of my sexual abuse and childhood trauma, my view of life was warped, which affected my relationships across the board. Exposure to sex at an early age normalized abnormal behaviors. According to *The Lifetime Prevalence of Child Sexual Abuse and Sexual Assault Assessed in Late Adolescence*,[1] one in nine girls and one in 53 boys under 18 experience sexual abuse or assault at the hands of an adult. As a child and throughout my teenage years, I believed everybody had sexual relationships. I believed that was how people acted, which should not have been the case. Since sex was a normalized behavior, I constantly operated in a space where it was yearned for and desired. I didn't understand that there was more to a connection outside of a physical attraction. Being mentally and emotionally connected to your partner was important for making them feel safe. There were times that sex gave me peace despite any mood or headspace I was in at the time. I didn't think of my actions as harmful because I wasn't fully comprehending the effects of my trauma. The desire for sex was there, but the understanding was not. When most people deal with challenges, they may turn to something for comfort, such as drugs, alcohol, or sex. I wasn't into drugs and alcohol, but sex was my thing. According

---

1   Finkelhor, David, Anne Shattuck, Heather A. Turner, and Sherry L. Hamby. 2014. "The Lifetime Prevalence of Child Sexual Abuse and Sexual Assault Assessed in Late Adolescence." *Journal of Adolescent Health* 55 (3): 329–33. https://doi.org/10.1016/j.jadohealth.2013.12.026.

to H.M. Zinzow, H.S., the effects of child sexual abuse can be long-lasting. Victims are more likely than non-victims to experience mental health challenges.

- Victims are about four times more likely to develop symptoms of drug abuse.
- Victims are about four times more likely to experience PTSD as adults.
- Victims are about three times more likely to experience a major depressive episode as adults.

Dealing with different women and engaging in sex is not as glamorous, fulfilling, or exciting as society leads you to believe. During those times, I felt off and had to slow myself down. At the time, these sexual encounters also led to an exchange of different energies. I was exhausted from entertaining multiple people, and the pointless conversations were vampire-like, draining the energy from my soul. Not to mention keeping up with lies was tiring and pushed me off track. As a student-athlete, staying focused and having your priorities in order are especially important. The same applies to adulthood, and my path was not conducive to productivity and focus.

As I got older, I realized that my lifestyle was not in the best interest of my growth and development. Now, I take time to breathe, read, do yoga, and meditate. So much energy was put into sex versus healthy outlets to feel peace. My younger self had no interest in those things and took a more reckless path to peace, such as entertaining different women, always on the hunt, and sometimes sleeping with multiple women on the same day.

You must be willing to peel that scab off to recover from childhood trauma. The thought of vulnerability scares many people because they do not want to face that dark side of their life. This is why people put up walls. They do whatever is needed to keep people at a distance because that is their way of protecting themselves. Putting up walls is not how to protect yourself because while those walls keep others out, they could also trap you.

Unlearn and relearn.

I now fully understand the importance of being vulnerable. Expressing yourself is a beautiful way to start your healing journey.

The more I addressed the trauma, the more I grew.

The more I grew, the stronger I became.

The stronger I became, the better I became at protecting myself and growing in healthy ways.

Now that life is on track, emotionally, mentally, and spiritually, I am enjoying a healthier version of myself. Who you listen to, what you follow, and the energy you surround yourself with greatly impact where you are going. Eventually, you may reach a point where toxicity is exhausting and debilitating. Those that have not embraced that reality will remain stuck, perhaps moving backward. It's a scary place to be when you don't understand the correct way to heal a wound. Balance is key –

accepting that everything and everyone is a learning experience with equal importance. I recognized that I no longer wanted to look at people sideways every day. I want to walk through life healed, optimistic, and sound. It's exhausting having to look over your shoulder all the time. So, I started doing the work and learning about myself. I fell in love with myself all over again and realized that what happened to me was not my fault.

Removing that pain, guilt, and brokenness was a game changer. My children deserved a better me, and I worked to do just that. I also wanted to experience healthier relationships. I stopped taking things personally and projecting other people's feelings onto me. Now, I see people for who they are while trying to understand the circumstances surrounding their makeup. My evolution as a man and experiences with emotional growth and subsequent emotional intelligence were changes I've fully embraced. In fact, emotional intelligence is something we don't talk about enough. Our ability to be aware of, control, communicate, show empathy, and handle relationships are components of high emotional intelligence. Looking back, I realize I acquired that later in life, but now that I am fully aware, I welcome opportunities to increase my emotional IQ. These new heights would not be possible without unpacking the trauma from my abuse.

I know some people may ask what the lesson is we learn from abuse. Well, I learned how I wanted to be treated by people in my life. I know what I am and am not willing to deal with from those individuals. Establishing boundaries is important. I learned the power of saying no, without feeling guilty. Understanding how to deal with my triggers was a big part of my growth, especially because I've seen the effects when not addressed. What happened to me was not my fault, which I eventually realized while learning the power of forgiveness and how to love. I became a better father and an overall better man. I had to take control of the narrative to use my story to help and heal. Even with this understanding, I have a long way to go.

Some of us have gone through more pain than others. When getting into a relationship, use your experiences to set boundaries and protect yourself while standing firm on those. Healthy boundaries mean taking responsibility for your actions and emotions and not taking responsibility for others' actions and emotions. Some of my boundaries include the following:

1. Saying no
2. Expecting respect
3. Refusing to take the blame for others' actions
4. Choosing to be vulnerable and never feeling pressured to open up
5. Understanding my right to privacy. What's mine is mine and my right to share or not share.

As you continue to grow and go on your life's journey, you learn what's acceptable for yourself and in relationships. Love looks different for each person. Unfortunately, to some, abuse looks like love. For example, she may say, "he beat me" or "she cussed me out," so they must love me. Many people think abuse is love because they grew up witnessing it in their household. They may be fooled by the illusion of love because their parents are still together, so they think it's okay. Additionally, society has normalized dysfunctional behavior, normalizing trauma and abuse. To avoid dysfunctional relationships, you must mentally outline your standards and boundaries and vow not to tolerate unhealthy behavior from yourself and others.

Repeat after me: I know my value and worth, and my decisions reflect self-love.

## Chapter Two

# DIVIDING LINES

*"Love yourself enough to set boundaries. Your time and energy are precious, and you can decide how to use them. You teach people how to treat you by deciding what you will and won't accept."*

Anna Taylor

WHAT DO HEALTHY BOUNDARIES LOOK like in a relationship? You must set boundaries with your partner to maintain a healthy and balanced relationship. Healthy and balanced relationships include respect, safety, trust, accountability, and support. If you've never seen or experienced this, knowing how to set certain boundaries for your relationship can be hard. One of the purposes of this book and this chapter is for you to take ownership. Boundaries and ownership are synonymous in healthy relationships, both leading to and creating mental and emotional stability.

*"Daring to set boundaries is about having the courage to love ourselves, even when we risk disappointing others."*

Brené Brown

Setting healthy boundaries means putting yourself in the healthiest possible situations. Healthy boundaries honor your moral code, comfortability, and love language. I want to be the best version of myself without losing who I am in the process due to overcompensating, people-pleasing, or doing things I wouldn't normally do just to make someone happy. People pleasing leads to resentment, insecurity, and unfulfillment. Plus, people-pleasing isn't usually a one-time thing. It becomes a pattern without any fulfillment in sight. Healthy boundaries establish accountability, communication, and respect. Despite having the tools in my emotional toolbelt to approach conflict, I always take a step back if toxicity appears. None of us are perfect, and as collected or sound as we may be, we can still benefit from a deep breath before approaching conflict. A negative situation, person, or circumstance may alter my feelings, mood, or response. Since I appreciate clear and respectful communication without the need to point fingers, I must enforce my boundary and pause before digging a deeper hole. After all, being disrespectful gets us nowhere. Instead, we should be in the correct mental and emotional space before engaging in challenging conversations. Your acknowledgment and understanding of personal boundaries are paramount. Without that understanding, your partner will not know the importance of your boundaries to avoid disrespectful or toxic situations.

I set healthy boundaries for myself by expressing past situations to my partner. I believe this is a great way of letting her know my past, and at the same time, there is context to the boundaries being set. Transparency unlocks new levels of closeness. For example, I may express something she doesn't like. She may take offense or can't accept it but using an example from a previous relationship and describing how it affected me could provide clarity for her. I feel it's helpful to understand better why I'm the way I am. This approach helped me in my relationships across the board, where I felt not ashamed or guilty about communicating my needs and thoughts. Be confident in expressing what's important to you.

Boundary setting and maintenance are necessary for healthy relationships. Expressing your beliefs and core values and holding yourself accountable is important, too. Core values guide you when making decisions and building relationships. Being led by integrity, respect, and responsibility steers me away from toxic relationships and keeps me on the path of peace.

Core values are important when expressing your boundaries while showing your partner how you value yourself and them as well. Although you express your feelings and communicate what's important in your life, you also consider how the other person may feel or view your thoughts. Due to childhood trauma, insecurities, or lack of healthy examples, some people may struggle with boundaries. So, growth is needed in that area to see eye to eye before getting into a space where you are heard or seen.

Personal beliefs and core values help each party understand one another. Beliefs and core values allow both parties to have open thoughts and the opportunity to articulate what they stand for. At the end of the day, male or female, it's important to understand that we all have emotions and may not always handle things in the best manner. Sometimes we can be selfish and only worry about our feelings, but it is important to look at both sides. Doing the work is necessary and a continuous process because we are always a work in progress. This work has helped me on my journey. Having that understanding has allowed me to be gracious and patient while developing the ability to forgive easily. I have the mindset that if this relationship is worth it, we'll figure it out in some shape or form. Sometimes that may come in the form of being the bigger person to protect the peace of both individuals. It does not mean that you must overextend yourself. Instead, do what feels comfortable and make sure your efforts are genuine. I make it my intention to move in love and light. Although I have my boundaries, grace is of the essence. Your significant other may cross boundaries many times; however, with love, humility, patience, and kindness, you will find a way.

I am very understanding of people's mental and emotional space, which makes me extremely patient in my relationships. Having a solid foundation when dealing with unresolved issues is vital. No one will agree with you 100% of the time, which is natural, but it is important to be heard and listen. Understanding each other's position is a starting point. If the situation is unresolved, it may be best to revisit the conversation later. For example, if I feel we cannot have a healthy conversation at that moment, I may suggest that we hold off until we are in a better space to talk and when emotions are settled. We must calm down to hear each other. If a person's actions are starting to shift negatively, I'll back up and give that person their space, allowing us to let the situation breathe. Lastly, I would like to point out that there are times when there isn't a resolution. In those cases, agree to disagree, but make sure that each side feels good about listening to each other's feelings. Again, listening and agreeing are two different things, but you want your partner to continue feeling good about coming to you. Some conversations may be difficult, but we must have the courage and confidence to engage in them.

*"Confidence is key, and not shying away from hard conversations is important."*

If you know what you want, simply express it and make sure to follow through with it. The concept is simple—stick to things that matter to you and ensure your partner understands their importance. If you don't stand up for yourself, who will? If you struggle with confidence, try talking yourself up with affirmations. Aim to build positive relationships with others. After all, we don't need anyone bringing us down. Being around people who are where you want to go or exemplify how you want to feel is beneficial. And don't forget about acts of self-care, too. Pour into yourself the way you would a loved one.

I have been through enough in my life, but I am now in a space to effectively communicate what I want in a relationship, friendship, business, and so forth. I want to be around solid people who love and appreciate me. If someone doesn't want that, cool, they are not a fit for me. You must speak confidently to that so the other person understands the importance of what matters to you. People have difficulty dealing with someone confident and in their own lane. That's not your concern. That does not mean I don't have my own struggles or that there aren't things I battle. I am growing and in a place where I am confident of my wants and needs. Unfortunately, I've been on the other side where people in my past have dealt with me because of who I am. Fake love is the worst. Through all that, I have learned to appreciate and forgive myself while understanding myself at the same time. I've seized opportunities to think through my wants, needs, thoughts, and feelings, and because of that, I cut the chaos from my life. That was huge for me. It doesn't matter if you are in a relationship or not—becoming your biggest fan is game-changing.

*"The boundary is there because when conflict arises, this will be the response for how it will be handled."*

Some of my boundaries consist of communication and respect, which come from a place of grace because I refuse to lose myself in a situation. Grace gives me an understanding of how to deal with people. In some relationships, I had to choose myself because the refusal to lose who I am took precedence over a particular situation or relationship. Some people do not understand boundaries and will cross the line repeatedly. So, it may be pointless to try getting through to them. In those situations, I've learned how to make choices to suit me best, but I understand this is different for everyone. How you carry yourself helps people identify your boundaries. It does not matter how close they are to you because your actions will dictate how they interact with you. For example, take a street guy. If he has a certain reputation, people typically won't mess with him. It's the same with boundaries and how a person carries themself.

*"Everyone's boundaries look different, and people must find what works for them."*

Setting boundaries keeps us grounded and ensures that we don't lose ourselves. We have to know our breaking points. Whatever your boundaries are, stand on them. They are put in place for a reason. You should not feel guilty about enforcing your expectations. What confuses people is when you say something one day but do something different the next day. This sends mixed messages. You must figure out what works for you and hold yourself accountable. Accountability is a lost art that people do not value and hold themselves to as they should. People look to others for love, and it shouldn't be like that. Be accountable and stand on your boundaries.

# Chapter Three

# CONNECTING DOTS

*"If you're going to start a new chapter, clarity is needed to begin."*

Josh Powell

T O BUILD A HOME, A strong, unshakable foundation is a must. If your foundation is not solid, your home will lack stability and eventually fall apart. Like a structural foundation, building a strong foundation in your relationships is very important, and clarity is a great way to begin. With clarity, you know exactly where the relationship is going. The framework is set, whether sexual in nature, a friendship, or building a monogamous relationship. You will know. To know, you must have important, transparent conversations, asking questions such as –

Where do you see this going?

What are your principles, morals, and values?

Do you have childhood trauma?

How do you handle conflict?

What are your goals and aspirations?

Where do you see yourself in five years?

I know people who were friends that fell deeply in love, got married within a year, and now live happily ever after. I also know people who were friends for years, but the relationship began to fall apart once they married. Instead of rushing to label the relationship, clarify your intentions with that individual. Clarity is especially important when building with someone. During the communication process and the getting-to-know-each-other phase, state what you want and what you are about, and stand on that. Do not make the mistake of telling the other person what they want to hear. Starting your foundation off that way is unstable, and you will cheat yourself in the end.

Assess what you want in life. Perhaps you want to be married, have kids, or continue on your spiritual walk. Well, it would only make sense to share those wants with whomever you seek to have in your life. Have those potentially uncomfortable conversations. Those conversations should happen immediately, too. People should know where you stand sooner rather than later. Don't play with others' time and emotions. Being strung along can cause unnecessary pain due to the lack of clarity. An understanding should come in the earliest stages so everyone is on the same page. That does not mean rushing into a relationship but knowing you both want the same things is a great start to building a solid foundation.

Having clarity and diving into those uncomfortable conversations does not exempt people from changing their minds. People change, but if they know your intentions and vice versa, change shouldn't be a problem because it will be communicated. Having that understanding and growing together is important.

What do women mostly complain about when it comes to men?

We play games and don't communicate.

Men, express your vision of the relationship. Lay it out for them through conversation and ask questions that complement your vision. Simply put, a question such as "Does what I shared match some of your thoughts" can provide answers leading to peace and clarity. When I meet someone, I ask questions like "What does dating/relationships look like for you?" I can't sugarcoat my past or the fact that I have children because that's a part of who I am. This dialogue is not a waste of time; it actually saves time. No time will be spent wondering, and honest conversations cut through all the bull and drama. Clarity helps to build that solid foundation. While securing your foundation, remain committed to learning about your potential partner. Effort should always be given because you certainly expect it, right? When the foundation is in place, continue to use those building blocks of communication, boundary setting, and confidence to grow with your person.

Although clarity is a plus, red flags and clarity go hand in hand because as you speak with others, you will learn about them, which may not always be pleasant. Clarity doesn't negate interactions. Clarity allows you to see things for what they are, which means pinpointing red flags, too. Red flags are signs that tell you something isn't right. Red flags can be different for everyone. Some red flags that stood out to me were controlling personalities; physically, mentally, and emotionally abusive tendencies; and anger management issues. You will pick up on red flags through conversations and time spent, and it's up to you to decide how to move forward. To save yourself from pain, never ignore how you feel regarding a person, situation, or circumstance. Pay close attention to your instincts when they kick in, and do your due diligence.

> *"I want people to see the value in themselves and realize it's not in a relationship, a house, or a car."*

Rejection prevents people from seeking clarity. People fear rejection, so they fear asking important questions while building a relationship. Sometimes we aren't willing to hear the truth and feel afraid that the person isn't for us. This is how you combat those feelings: Believe you are an amazing person. Love yourself and know that you are enough. Sometimes we aren't a fit for that person, but that's okay. Your value isn't based on a relationship or circumstance. It also does not mean you are not worthy of being treated how you desire. You cannot allow one person to kill your spirit because ten other people to that one will appreciate you and love you for you. Unfortunately, that one person will stick out like a sore thumb, and many times, we have a tough time getting past that person. Naturally, we want people to like us. We want people to see our value and appreciate it. So, your feelings may feel crushed when someone doesn't agree or feel the same way about you. That puts people in the mind frame of thinking about what they could do to    change their minds, which goes back to people pleasing. The truth is you can't please everyone. Through growth and maturity, though, those truths become more digestible. What's for you is for you, and what's meant for you will come when there is a shift in your focus and mentality.

There is also power in the tongue. Bring positive energy to yourself through your thoughts and words. How you think about yourself is another part of clarity. Regardless of who accepts and supports me, I'll be good if my phone stops ringing today. I wouldn't feel like less of a person because those things don't take away from who I am. I will show up every day and do the best that I can. It's a blessing when you have an opportunity to be in a person's presence. That is why I don't feel like I'm being cocky when I say it's a privilege to be in mine. Despite the things I've gone through, I truly believe in myself. I pick and choose who I allow around me. Despite all the strides I have made, there are still many things that I need to work on and improve. We all do, right? I know my value as a person, so if a relationship costs me my peace, that relationship will be removed. We all should be aware of the value of protecting ourselves.

Dive into affirmations to improve your self-esteem. With so much going on each day, reminding yourself of your value is important. The following are affirmations I recite daily. I hope they serve you well:

I love you.

I am worthy.

I matter.

I am enough.

I am growing.

I trust the process.

*Emotional Over Physical*

*"Lust shouts. Love whispers. Only the heart knows the difference."*

Jan Hurst-Nicholson

When it comes to love or lust, do not play about your intentions for someone when dealing with them. Not every interaction must lead to a serious relationship. People form business partnerships and become acquaintances, friends, or romantic partners. For the most part, you should know your intentions. As adults, we should be able to distinguish the path of the relationship, if any.

When it comes to sexual relationships, people operate by different rulebooks. Personally, I am very big on connection, whereas others may be led by beliefs and feelings. When there is a genuine connection, though, intimacy often follows. Despite connection and chemistry, conversation and transparency remain key points to a healthy relationship. It's very important to ensure that both people are on the same page. As grounded, healthy-minded adults, we are responsible for discussing the relationship's effects once sex is brought into the picture. Regardless of the timing, whether a week, four to six months or after you tie the knot, there will be a shift because sex changes the relationship. If you choose to lay with someone, you also need to choose to communicate with them effectively. Discuss expectations because there may be awkwardness after sex. The other person may wonder if you'll call the next day or where you stand. This insight speaks to those engaging in sexual-based relationships instead of building a foundation with one individual.

People need reassurance, especially when sex has been introduced in the relationship. Fellas, make her feel safe and secure: "I know we just had sex, but I still want to build with you!" Be open and honest: "I still see an us and want to be with you." Put that out there so she knows. If you feel differently, say that, too. Even if you feel indifferent, there may be something you can work on because everyone's love language is not the same. Everyone's journey is different. Notably, life does not always go as planned, either. Show yourself grace for your decisions and stand firm in your choices.

As a Believer who began a deeper dive into spirituality, I realize that my decisions would have been significantly different had I exercised this level of maturity and understanding at a younger age. I would have moved differently, communicated differently, and viewed relationships differently. As the saying goes, "When you know better, you do better." Today, I make decisions that align with my belief system and values. No two journeys are alike; we should remember that before judging others.

> *"Love talks and talks. Lust is brief and to the point."*
>
> Mason Cooley

In a perfect world, people can spot their soulmate a mile away and skip the heartache of dating the wrong people. There are happily-ever-after instances, though, of people who see or meet someone for the first time and know that's their future spouse. Realistically, you may get that feeling when you get to know another person. Within two to three weeks of getting to know a person and feeling out the vibe between us, I can honestly say whether that person could be right for me. Being intentional helps get to the point. Intentionality allows us to sort through topics that could be difficult to discuss later when feelings are deeper. Typically, no one likes rocking the boat, especially when they feel things are going well. I would rather have some swaying versus a sunken boat, sunken meaning a disconnect from my emotional, mental, and spiritual well-being.

There is a lot of damage that could be done during the dating phase if we are not careful, and many of us fail to understand this. Some start questioning themselves and their worth due to bad experiences. Again, that is why clarity is key. Identifying red flags is key. Establishing boundaries is key. Otherwise, people will have you out here questioning love, not knowing what's real. They can tell you everything you want to hear and even act on it. Some can do this for a long time until they get what they want. Can you tell the difference? Is it love, or is it lust? Is it real, or is it not? Do you have what it takes to make the proper decision when need be? Take a look at these simple yet impactful pieces of insight to help you distinguish the differences:

- The other person values how you want to be treated, especially during trying times.
- When a challenge arises, you appreciate and respect their behavior.

- When the topic shifts from sex, they remain engaged and attentive.
- Intentions are never in question; safety is innately felt.

Therefore, the connection needs to be clear when deciding on moving forward.

## Chapter Four

# HEAD VS. HEART

*"Don't remove the emotion because that's the connection to the situation or person."*

Josh Powell

D O NOT ALLOW YOUR EMOTIONS to control you. The way to eliminate that issue is to grow and evolve in expressing emotion. Of course, feelings are important to honor and acknowledge, but the best decisions are rarely made during times of heightened feelings. Thinking logically benefits you in the long run, but choosing wisely in the now is not always easy. Most of the time, people will make the situation about them when two parties are involved. Your feelings are valid, but there is another person involved, too. What are their feelings about the situation? Their feelings have validity as well. Acknowledgment and sympathy must be fair across the board. Even if you don't agree with the other person, acknowledging their feelings is necessary to continue a healthy relationship and healthy communication habits.

"I said what I said."

"You should agree with me."

"You just don't understand."

Those are one-sided statements that lead to unbalanced conversations. The conversation was already going the wrong way, but now you made a hard detour down an emotional path. The argument has shifted to "Now you don't agree with what I am saying." This happens when you don't comprehend that person's feelings or emotions. This lack of understanding could lead to emotional triggers that sidetrack a conversation.

Remaining emotionally sound is not the same as not having or showing emotion. Feeling numb or overly emotionally led can be costly. I've come from that unemotional space, and it's not a healthy place. I learned to function in dysfunction, not realizing that shouldn't be the norm. Processing feelings are the norm. Understanding and learning how to express feelings is the norm. Feeling altogether is the norm. Instead, throughout the dysfunction, I believed this was just another day, and this was life. I expected to get hurt, and I expected the worst from situations. Bracing for the worst or expecting it should not be the standard. Although no one is exempt from experiencing pain and misfortune, everyone is entitled to process their feelings healthily.

Let's switch gears for a moment, though. In basketball, if we are in a big game and someone hard fouls me but the referee does not blow their whistle, there are a couple of ways to react. Think about the answers to the following—

What if I get wrapped up in my emotions and get thrown out of the game?

What if my reaction costs us the game?

What would happen if I kept my cool?

If I explode, perhaps my response is justified by the poor call, but I could cost my team the game. If I make it about me, the team will suffer. Our relationships can bear the same results. During difficult moments, it's easy to forget you and your partner are a team because it's easier to think about yourself when directly affected. Emotional defenses typically don't work out well, so it's probably best to avoid them. Instead, think before you speak and respond respectfully yet thoughtfully.

Reaching a point of respectful communication is why we must put in the work to understand that decision-making is critical in problem-solving. Emotions can cause us to make decisions we will later regret if not careful. Consider revisiting the situation when clearer and cooler heads prevail. Once the issues are addressed, there must be an understanding of what needs to be accomplished.

When hurt, people act and behave in damaging ways. In some cases, lashing out is a clear indication of hurt. Even though we have a right to our feelings, those feelings do not justify disrespect. Depending on the situation, I will continuously show up for that person, no matter what, and that's the hard part, especially amid hurt. Imagine doing that, being led by emotion. Lead by rationale by taking the following approaches:

- Think of the other person; step in their shoes to better empathize with their point of view.
- Explore different solutions to your problem, acknowledging that your way is not the only way to solve an issue.
- Make decisions to benefit you in the long run, not just at the moment.
- Do not make decisions while crying, heartbroken, frustrated, or furious; wait until you are in a peaceful space.

*"Do you want to know if you're growing? Let someone disrespect you, and you still follow through because that's in your spirit."*

Removing your emotions from challenging situations isn't easy. Take a married couple who has been together for a while. Over time, their spouse may do things that aggravate them. Even the sight of them can make one sick. Things that aren't being done become a bigger issue. Simple things like a sock on the floor can be annoying to the point of snapping. How many people will get a divorce if they allow moments like that to take over? I suggest removing yourself and thinking about everything before you act or speak. Relationships and marriages would last longer if more people did this versus splitting based on emotion and regretting it later. Whether it works or not, those steps are necessary. Walking away isn't the only option, though. For those that have "been there, done that," consider the following:

- Focus on your part in the situation and how to improve.
- Think before you speak, deciding how to lead by example to show your partner your effort.
- Post-argument, write how you feel to process your feelings and move on amicably.
- Suggest going for a walk together to calm your spirits and discussing in a neutral area.

Consider utilizing relationship counselors to help you on your journey of happiness. Counselors are a great resource to tap into when wanting to create healthy habits, work through issues, and maintain happiness. There is a misconception that counseling is only useful to tackle problems. However, counseling is great for maintenance, like cars get an oil change to maintain the engine. The way cars need maintenance is the same way relationships need continual care, too.

In past relationships, I tried to make them successful. My effort consisted of therapy, accountability, effort, growth, and letting go of the past, to name a few. We both played a role in how the relationship ended, but I asked for forgiveness and constantly worked on being a better version of myself for my family. Despite being in the midst of a divorce, I made another attempt to patch things up. I let some time pass but made another effort to do so after being baptized. I asked her, "Are you willing to let everything go to move forward in our relationship?" I let the past go and forgave, but the feeling wasn't mutual. At the end of the day, I am at peace with my decisions. I gave it my all and was able to move forward.

Today, healthy relationships look and feel different for me, including my relationship with self. As you grow, you should want a partner that's going in the same direction as you're going. Perhaps they aren't quite in the same space, but they're making an effort to become the best version of themselves. The key word is effort. Becoming your best self attracts that which is meant for you and loses those who do not serve you and your journey.

Purposeful, meaningful, and intentional relationships are the only relationships I seek to create and maintain, whether with family, friends, personal, or business. Second-guessing is exhausting, and I no longer have the capacity for it. That is why personal growth is key to having the relationships you desire. It starts with you. A healthier you won't allow half the things you did in the past. This is where recognizing green flags come into play. Green flags are positive attributes you notice in a person that spark peace within your soul, such as:

- They support your personal growth.
- They honor your boundaries.
- They openly communicate, remain vulnerable with you, and hold themselves accountable for their actions.
- They practice self-care and show an interest in personal elevation.
- They welcome tough conversations without cursing, yelling, and disrespectful tendencies.
- They want to see you win.

There are many more green flags, but those are excellent examples. Keep in mind that healthy relationships look like fighting for each other and not against each other because you both want the same things.

When coming together with someone while building a relationship, discussing your emotions and learning about each other daily is important. This is a crucial part of building. Having discussions about what triggers you and how to manage emotions is necessary. Explain your feelings to that person and discuss the importance of conflict resolution. Always be mindful that we must understand the bigger picture in those moments – enjoying one another's company, building something strong, and working toward establishing a future together. You are building with someone, yes, but how your partner wants to be loved is of great importance and should be discussed. Getting everything out in the open at the start is key. "Let me know your thoughts" is a simple yet efficient way of getting things underway in a relationship. Soon, you will be able to tackle difficult discussions more easily because your communication patterns are established and upheld.

## Chapter Five

# AT WHAT COST

*"Live so that when your children think of fairness
and integrity, they think of you."*

H. Jackson Brown, Jr.

ARE YOU ONE OF THE many diving into self-care and self-improvement? If you answered "yes," the fact that you're taking the time to work on yourself lets me know you love yourself. Diving into self-care does not mean you achieved your best self; it means you care to take the time to improve, recharge, re-evaluate, and elevate. Prioritizing your mental, emotional, and physical health shows you care about your life.

It also shows that you care about your relationships because you refuse to "pour from an empty cup," as the saying goes.

Focusing on your mental health is vital because your mental health impacts your thoughts, emotions, and behaviors. A healthy mindset promotes productivity and effectiveness in many areas of your life, including your relationships with yourself and others. There are many ways to actively work on your mental health. Each person finds comfort in different strategies, but a few ways to improve mental health are staying active, talking to a trusted loved one, getting proper sleep, and eating a healthy diet. I feel at my best when I enjoy all four. When I show up as my best self, my relationships also experience the best side of me.

Staying active has a major impact on your mental health. Body movement helps you rest better, is a great stress reliever, and helps improve your memory. Physical health has always been a part of my self-improvement journey. Even though my career required me to be in shape, I did not just work out for job purposes. Exercise helps to balance my emotions, gives me a good release whenever my feelings happen to be all over the place, and calms my mind. I remember many times when my heart was heavy, and I headed to the gym or enjoyed a yoga session, only to experience relief and gratitude. In a sense, whatever it was that had me upset was no longer so burdensome because putting my body in motion released so many stressors and pent-up feelings.

Speaking of pent-up feelings, talking to someone is also important for your mental health and creating good habits. Many times, when this is suggested, people's minds jump to therapy. Truth be told, I am a big advocate of therapy; however, that is not the only way of releasing your thoughts and feelings. Having someone you trust and care about is a great way to calm yourself and relieve stress. However, be mindful of whom you talk to about your thoughts, feelings, and problems. Not everyone is your friend. As harsh as that may seem, those words are true, and for you to create and maintain safe spaces in your life, you must discern who should be on the receiving end of your conversations. When you're in the company of someone solid, your gut should tell you. You will feel at ease, doubt will leave your mind, and you will be open to sharing what's on your heart. Coupling this with a therapist is ideal for mental health. Remember – you don't have to seek therapy for a particular issue or crisis. Therapy is an effective way to manage your life in a healthy way. Therapists are trained and educated professionals equipped to share advice, weigh in on your life, and find healthy solutions for your challenges. Although you may have a supportive, trusted circle of loved ones, therapists provide professionalism and experience that even the best of friends are ill-equipped to do.

On your mental health journey, which is truly ongoing, do not underestimate the value of proper rest. Between exercise, therapy, and time for self, sleep is key to recharging your battery. Without enough sleep, you cannot expect your brain to function properly. Keep in mind that resting and sleep are not the same. Sitting in bed and scrolling on your phone is not rest, especially before bedtime. Studies show that limiting your screen time has health benefits. Consider making changes and, instead, read a book to calm your mind, meditate, or write in a journal. When you wake up the next morning, your mind and body are in sync, and you're more inclined to make better decisions.

Consistent exercise filters into your sleep patterns as well as your food choices. However, you can exercise and sleep all you want, but without healthy eating habits, you are cheating your mind and body from outstanding health. Food affects our mood and mental health. Eating right is not only better for your health but also improves one's mood and mindset. According to Aetna.com, a Medicare provider, the link between diet and emotions stems from the relationship between your brain and gastrointestinal tract (GI tract), and the GI tract is often referred to as the "second brain."[2] The GI tract is home to countless bacteria that affect the production of chemicals that send messages from the stomach to the brain, including dopamine and serotonin. Eating natural, nutritionally dense foods promotes the growth of good bacteria, which positively affects chemical production. When production is at its best, your mind becomes clear, and your mood remains stable. So, you

---

2  Gomstyn, Alice. 2019. "Food for Your Mood: How What You Eat Affects Your Mental Health." Aetna. Aetna. 2019. https://www.aetna.com/health-guide/food-affects-mental-health.html.

can imagine what happens when "bad" bacteria enter the GI tract. High-sugar foods, especially, create temporary highs but those highs are followed by sudden crashes that immediately impact your feelings and bodily functions. Opt for foods with an ingredient list, such as vegetables, fruits, and so forth. Feed your belly to feed your brain, and watch your mind soar.

The mental health journey is not a destination but a lifetime process. We are forever evolving; therefore, we must be patient with ourselves. Two steps forward and one step back is not unusual. Do not beat yourself up for making grand plans to eat and sleep better but falling short. Each moment is a new chance to create change and improve. Take responsibility for your feelings and pay attention to your behavioral patterns. Treat yourself with kindness and respect. Think of how you speak to your best friend. Consider talking to yourself in the same manner by giving yourself grace. We all should value ourselves, right? Of course. A part of valuing yourself and doing the work is also celebrating the positives. Acknowledge growth and celebrate your wins, big and small.

Doing the work also means not allowing certain factors to trigger you, such as factors you can't control or change. Every day, people make choices. Some of these choices have a minimal effect on you, but some are crucial to moving forward in life. Choices like "if" or "how" to heal are important. Sometimes, people would rather lock away an issue than properly heal what ails them. How should I handle adversity? How do I put myself first? These are questions that are asked more often than you think by people who are trying to heal.

As you grow, you become better at observing, getting to the bottom of your issues, and refusing to make excuses. In my experience, most people justify their behavior and explain why they are the way they are instead of diving into life-changing habits. Some people have a challenging time with accountability and realizing that they could be the source of the problem. Taking the time to learn about yourself is essential for healing. Never take that process lightly. On the flip side, it's the same for people who make choices but fail to get help and take steps toward being better people. They usually find excuses for why they can't make the time despite its importance. You can tell you have healed or are healing by how you respond to a person or situation. When you make decisions to operate differently, you inevitably handle yourself in a more mature manner. Growth helps you understand your part in every situation in your life. You stop blaming others and pointing the finger.

Do the work! Do not allow outside noise, people, or mess to interfere with your journey. When you work on yourself, you will realize who deserves your time and space versus who does not.

## Chapter Six

# BUILDING BRIDGES

*"I want to build a relationship with someone who cares about 'why' I've been quiet all day, not someone who gets mad 'cause I'm 'acting' different."*

Unknown

THE PURPOSE OF BUILDING A bridge is to connect two sides. Without a bridge, people may remain stranded, unable to reach the other side. The same concept applies to relationships. We build bridges to connect emotionally, spiritually, mentally, and physically.

There are many ways to build bridges in a relationship, including removing your ego and me-first mentality and putting your partner first. Removing yourself has several meanings. First, this means no longer only looking at the situation from your side and your side only. Imagine if a bridge was constructed, but the architects only researched one side of the land. Chances are the bridge would be incomplete and nonfunctional.

Regarding relationships, building your bridge and removing yourself also means refocusing on your partner to learn everything about them. Learning what they like is the easy part. In most relationships, we quickly learn what our partners like, so we cater to them with those favorable things, yet we neglect the dislikes. Those dislikes, though, are where we gain a better understanding of their core. This level of effort and understanding contributes to a sturdier foundation and overall better structure. So, aim to learn what triggers your partner, the trauma they experienced, what bothers them, and their insecurities. Knowing those will help you understand your partner. You must learn and understand their fears as well. Dive deep with your significant other and learn how to love them. It's less about giving them what they want in a tangible sense and more about understanding what they need. Love based on wants seems beneficial, yet it only creates a surface level of love. You want to dive deep, past the surface, and be the supportive partner your other half needs and wants.

Beyond learning your partner, commit to learning your partner's family background and dynamic and how they function as a unit. How does your partner think and process thoughts? From where did they get their morals, values, and beliefs? My experiences, trials, tribulations, therapy, traveling, watching other cultures, and being a part of other traditions helped shape and mold me over the years.

I learned many lessons from the diverse cultures I immersed myself in, along with new ideas and confirmation through conversations I've had in each country. While living In Korea, for example, I learned that a man's role is largely important outside the home – making money to provide and protect – whereas a woman's role is inside the house, taking care of the kids and housework. Although rules have changed in recent years, these are still prevalent in Korean culture. As a result of my time spent in Korea, my outlook has been developed and broadened, yet my experiences differ from others, including my partner. These experiences taught me what successful relationships look like in other areas of the world. I was able to have real discussions with families and dive into their mindsets. Culture is important and has shown me how people view relationships in other countries. These rich experiences have helped shape my mentality as it pertains to relationships. It gave me a fresh outlook on how we can grow as people and what our priorities should be when building with our partners.

I like to study my partner as we build together, which is a constant learning process. It helps bridge the gap regarding our differences. I analyze the details about her that will enable me to be the best I can be for her. You will understand how to operate in different situations by learning the fine details. One of the many situations we face is conflict. Conflict arises for many reasons during a relationship. Conflict will test your relationship the most, so having a strong foundation is important. You will better understand how to operate in your household in a healthy space and pick up the signs when something is wrong with your partner. Building a natural bond creates a deeper connection. The work must be consistent. Learning about your partner and gaining a better understanding helps you navigate those difficult times in the relationship.

Have you ever misread your partner's body language? How did it feel when your partner misread yours? Most people will take body language and run with it. Even if someone is right with their thoughts, it could still be frustrating when not given an opportunity to express your feelings. Assuming leads to arguments and misinterpretations, so we should always clearly address the issue at hand. For example, if she's not talking, I could assume something may be bothering her. Assumption will allow you to think that her problem is with you. Instead of forming misguided opinions, ask her if everything is okay. Give her a space where she is comfortable expressing herself. I want to do everything in my power to bring my partner and me closer. Understanding her mood swings, not taking her attitudes personally, and bringing calm amid conflict are just a few ways. Instead of letting emotions run wild, I am now able to stay calm and manage the situation with grace and love. This is one of the hidden secrets to a relationship. Filling up your partner's love tank is more than doing the things they like. How you handle yourself during a time of conflict goes a long way.

I'm very big on love languages. Consider reading *The 5 Love Languages* by Gary Chapman, a book that has changed the communication styles of individuals and couples across the world. For those who may not know the love languages, here is the list of the five love languages:

- Words of Affirmation – encouragement, affirmation, and appreciation
- Physical Touch – non-verbal use of body language and touch
- Receiving Gifts – thoughtfulness and making your partner a priority
- Quality Time – uninterrupted and focused one-on-one time
- Acts of Service – wanting to help your partner to lighten their load

Learning my partner's love language is a priority. You need to know your partner's love language to help you better love and understand them. Loving your partner the way they want to be loved versus how you feel they should be loved is key. I believe that's a common mistake many make. Then, people wonder why there is a disconnect. In a relationship, we continue doing what we want and not what serves our partner.

In most cases, your partner will not just tell their love language; that is where learning your partner comes into play. To understand their needs, you must do the work. Your partner may not want to share that or even know how. We're always looking for a quick fix instead of trying to understand our partners better. We don't want problems, but if you love that person, you'll try to heal the wounds instead of putting a bandage on the problem. To illustrate my point – "Oh, she's upset, let me take her shopping" is putting a bandage on the situation. The better approach is the direct questioning of what is wrong, hugging her, and trying to figure out the solution. Sometimes she may not be willing to divulge, but in those moments, I must figure out ways for her to open up. Suggestions like therapy where a neutral party is involved may prove helpful in creating more transparency. It could help ease her mind and be more open to discussing issues. That is the length we must go to better understand our partners and how to work through issues. We should be able to put our pride and ego to the side and figure out how to connect. The deeper the connection, the better.

When building a bridge, safety and structure are key. Similarly, women want to feel safe, too. When she feels safe, you unlock a door of love on another level that allows her to be who she is truly meant to be. That's power within itself. Parimala Tadas wrote in her 2019 article *Essence of Being a Woman* that a woman is an affectionate mother, a devoted wife, a caring daughter, a trustworthy sister, and a loyal friend. In a true sense, a woman is the very existence of nature. She is Shakti and the very embodiment of supreme energy. A woman personifies ageless beauty, selfless love, purity, grace, and dignity. Many women love their partners but don't necessarily feel safe with them. She can be head over heels for him yet uncomfortable communicating a problem that may exist. She could be scared to communicate when something bothers her. It is your job to make your partner feel safe so that they can express their needs. This is a part of building bridges.

## Chapter Seven

# SAME TEAM

*"The happiest relationships are those where you're a team, where you protect each other and stand up for one another."*

Unknown

As MANY ALREADY KNOW, A team is a group; people that join forces in unity. When I think of a group of people that join forces in unity, the athlete in me immediately thinks of championship teams that achieved the ultimate goal (winning at the highest level). The Golden State Warriors and the Bulls during the Jordan era come to mind. These teams won championships because they were on the same page. They had the same goal. They tapped into one another's strengths and made up for one another's weaknesses. I encourage you to consider your relationship as a team. It's a blessing when two committed people work together to see the relationship succeed. It's a good feeling to have mutual support and togetherness. So, when discussing your relationship, you must look at everything from an "us" or "we" standpoint versus an "I" or "me" standpoint. Even the best athletes in the game have an us-centered mentality. Without that, they cannot succeed.

Teams run into issues regardless of talent, skill, or us-centered mentality. Concerning my partner, I've learned that my communication must be expressed properly if we face a struggle. The discussion must be about how we can better serve one another. I can't make the situation about me. That's easier said than done, though, especially when emotions are involved. So, how should you approach sensitive situations or heightened emotions?

- Give the situation time before talking about it with your partner. That's not to say you should disappear or remain silent. Instead, express that you are taking a breather, and set a time to chat when you feel centered and focused on solutions instead of your emotions.
- During that pause, take the time to understand your partner's concerns. Finding solutions means understanding your feelings as well as their feelings.

This creates a culture in your relationship centered around understanding and grace.

- Be mindful of tone. The proper tone is important because you want to be heard, remain respectful, and continue to create that culture of understanding. Leave condescending words and demeaning nature at the door.
- When expressing yourself, stay away from finger-pointing, shaming, and guilt-tripping.
- Remember: You are a team, and working together on a solution is the goal.

I will not drag my partner through the mud because I need them to agree with my feelings. During a disagreement, one person often focuses on their feelings while neglecting their partner's feelings. That is I-centered, not us-centered. When this happens, your thoughts fall on deaf ears. Nobody wins. Remember – successful couples fight for each other and not against one another. Think of the overall picture despite your feelings at the moment. The overall picture is harmony, respect, and love. That's not to say you should dismiss your feelings for the sake of harmony. Instead, choose to communicate in a healthy manner. Keep this gem in mind: How you articulate something makes all the difference. For example, a small situation could become bigger if not communicated thoughtfully. If I didn't like a particular dish that my partner made, I might say, "Hey, may I suggest something for the next time you make this dish?" That's a small example but something that may hurt your partner's feelings if not approached with consideration. Therefore, in expressing my displeasure, I need to keep that in mind. What I'm saying and what she's hearing are two different things. I'm only expressing my thoughts on that one dish. She could interpret that as I'm not pleased when she cooks. With that being said, my tone helps me to be heard. Delivery matters. I do not want her to feel disrespected or unhappy. I just didn't like something and wanted to address it in a way that resonated with her to create change instead of sparking a fight.

Arguments, although uncomfortable, lead to understanding if communication remains at the forefront. How can we resolve this issue? That is the mentality to keep in mind. Steer clear of being the party that wants the other to understand and agree with how they feel, and that's that. That one-sided communication leads to a worse argument when the argument should be a conversation used for understanding. Keep in mind that you can have a passionate discussion without arguing. When people argue, they only want to be right or heard. In enters the ego. When an argument ensues, it doesn't matter what the other person feels or thinks because ego overrules all. Bring yourself back to the us-mentality. If I'm willing to have a conversation, I am not only willing to express myself but also to hear what you have to say. That is what teamwork is all about.

If you finish a discussion with your partner and only one side is heard, that's a loss.

If you finish a discussion with your partner and there is no resolution, that's a loss.

If you finish a discussion with your partner and they do not express their thoughts, that's a loss.

That is why I stress the importance of being on the same team, being there for one another, and having that shared understanding. I want to hear my partner while removing my emotions from the conversation. Understanding my partner helps us. It helps me to understand how to move forward and tap into her needs; in turn, that will make her feel better in the relationship, which makes us better. A disagreement is not a competition between us if we're on the same team.

How can you say you're on the same team when you can't express something the other person needs to hear?

How can you say you're on the same team but don't feel comfortable being vulnerable with your partner?

How can you say you're on the same team when you don't feel safe with your partner?

The foundation is crucial for having that understanding, being on the same page, and wanting the same things. You and your partner should have the same mentality when building your foundation. If you agree to communicate a certain way (for example – not raising voices during conversation), that's a great addition to your relationship's foundation. Go in the same direction as one another – same path, same pace. You can go farther together.

## Chapter Eight

# EXONERATION

*"Forgiveness does not change the past, but it does enlarge the future."*

Paul Boose

N<small>O MATTER HOW LONG YOU</small> have been with your partner or spouse, forgiveness will play a role in your relationship, but that's not always to say forgiveness will play a positive role. This is very much dependent on how each person views forgiveness and gives it. If one person decides to harbor resentment, feel anger, and not prioritize letting go, the relationship will more than likely be short-lived. On the other hand, when forgiveness is exercised, longevity will follow. Throughout life, you must learn to forgive your friends, family, and yourself. Otherwise, relationships will only go so far.

Starting with self-forgiveness is vital. Holding on to resentment can increase stress levels and takes a toll on our well-being. We've been taught to believe that we need to be hard on ourselves for us to take responsibility for our actions. This mindset can sabotage our efforts to lead meaningful, happy, fulfilling lives. We can always learn and mature through our mistakes.

> *"There is no love without forgiveness, and there is no forgiveness without love."*
>
> Bryant McGill

Self-forgiveness empowers you to take responsibility for your words and behaviors. Forgiveness should promote a shift from self-blame to responsibility. Forgiving yourself allows you to stop looking at yourself as a victim or someone who does people wrong. Regain your confidence to abandon those thoughts and believe in yourself again. With self-forgiveness, you can start learning to identify negative thoughts and emotions. Over time, you should be able to replace those thoughts and emotions with compassion and love for yourself. When forgiving yourself, you should reflect on your feelings. Face what happened and accept responsibility for it.

Forgiving yourself and others may seem inconceivable, maybe even impossible. Still, I always forgive the person regardless of if they apologized because I don't want to give them power over me. It's especially important to forgive so the healing process can begin for you and your relationship. That's not to say I'm excusing what was done or how it made me feel because I will still go through those emotions. Despite those feelings, I can't stay stuck in those feelings. I need to be able to move forward and process correctly. Forgiveness is just as important for you as it is for your partner.

> *"You forgive people based on who you are and how you move. You can choose to handle the situation according to what you feel is best for you."*

For some, forgiveness could look like staying, leaving, or taking time for themselves. It depends on the act and what happened. I don't base my decision on the person or what they did. I must do what's best for me but ensure that forgiveness, not anger, is my starting point. I do my best to process the situation and let go of what happened so I can move forward. Most people pick and choose when they want to be loving, caring, kind, and forgiving. When they are the offender, those same people want you to immediately process all of your emotions and extend grace, something they are unwilling to give. It's interesting how quickly they would like the other person to forgive and forget immediately. They want you to move on from the offense and not bring it up anymore, which isn't right or fair.

Unforgiveness can eat away at you. Those thoughts can creep up on you and instantly shift your mood to a dark place of depression, shame, and guilt. That's why I rely heavily on the presence of God to shield me from attacks on my mind and heart to heal from the offense. Trusting in the Creator strengthens you to understand that it's not as bad as it looks. I look at the situation and ask God a few important questions:

- What did You want me to gain from this experience?
- What is it that You want me to learn from this experience?
- Why did this experience have to happen?

I'll be honest—I don't always get the answers, but I gain peace because I know God has a greater plan for me. God uses each lesson to build me up, strengthen me, and prepare me for something greater. Once I realized that, it helped me begin the process of healing and letting go of the pain. Learning to gain a greater perspective on a challenging situation helps you overcome negative feelings and move on to a greater future.

*"Love is patient, love is kind. It does not envy, it does not boast, it is not proud. It does not dishonor others, it is not self-seeking, it is not*

*easily angered, it keeps no record of wrongs. Love does not delight in evil but rejoices with the truth. It always protects, always trusts, always hopes, always perseveres."*

1 Corinthians 13:4-7 (NIV)

This verse is love in its essence. This is grace. This is forgiveness. This is all of that and then some. This is God's love, not our love. Our love allows our pride and ego to get in the way. Our love does not always forgive, forgive easily, or let go. Our love makes us selfish and only see one-sided. Our love does not put others first. Our love has it that our only concern is us and that love will choose self over everything most of the time.

So many people want grace given to them, but they're not willing to extend grace to anyone. Yes, in a relationship, people will hurt you, things will happen, and there's nothing you can do to avoid that. That's why we can make decisions on how we choose to deal with that person moving forward. I know and understand there are deal breakers. Even in those moments, you can still forgive the person who offended you. For example: A man puts his hands on a woman, which is the basis for an immediate exit, and she chooses to forgive him. Let's say she stays in the relationship, and the behavior continues. Now she is faced with a decision. Whether she leaves is a separate matter.

I don't condone anyone putting hands on each other, but forgiveness is the key to starting her healing process. Remember

– forgiveness is just as important to your emotional and mental health as it is for your partner.

People have opinions on how they would like to move forward when it comes to cheating. Some people are one and done, whereas others may stay. For some, their decision depends on the situation and history. No matter what has been done, we can choose how we want to move forward. Although other people will weigh in on your life, never forget that the ultimate decision rests with you. No matter what you choose, whether you stay in the relationship or leave, forgiveness is a great starting point. Forgiving the person and how you move forward are two different things. Forgiveness is taking your power back and not giving it away.

A person could try hard to get back in your good graces, but their efforts would never be recognized because they haven't been forgiven. People may say they have forgiven you yet harbor pain and resentment. We don't speak about that enough. Many relationships are ruined because people decide not to forgive, forget, and move on. Those same people, when on the other end, would like their partner to move on and move forward graciously.

Another reason I forgive the way I do is because I understand that unforgiveness silently kills us. It is unhealthy to harbor pain, negative feelings, and brokenness. It's unhealthy to hold on to the act that was committed. Lastly, forgiveness doesn't always mean you stay, either. If you claim to love someone or want to continue moving forward with that person, you must make some tough decisions. I'm not saying forgiveness is easy, but it's worth it.

I'm not saying that once you forgive someone you will live happily ever after, but you have a choice with how you process your emotions. You're helping yourself by forgiving. Forgiveness should start with you, which we don't do enough of. We want to point the finger at the other person, but let's look at ourselves first. Didn't we choose the person or the situation? Didn't we stay despite what they showed us? I don't like harping on or continuing to hold on to things because it bleeds onto other aspects of your life. Many people carry baggage from past relationships that they haven't forgiven and bring into new situations. Many times, in past relationships, my partner was triggered, and it had nothing to do with me. Ultimately, I became the person who received negative, unwarranted energy. That is why doing the work and letting things go are important. Otherwise, we will kill a relationship by hanging on to childhood trauma, our first heartbreak, or that one bad relationship. An amazing person can come into your life, and you won't be ready for them because you didn't properly heal and are holding on to past issues. Do the work and forgive because negative feelings are detrimental to your health and well-being.

*"True forgiveness is when you can say thank you for that experience."*

Oprah Winfrey

Beyond the word "love," many words, especially in the Bible, reflect love and forgiveness – grace and mercy being two of those words. Grace, as shared in the Bible and understood by Christians, is a spontaneous gift from God that takes the form of divine favor, love, compassion, and a share in the divine life of God. Grace is an attribute of God that is most manifested in the salvation of sinners. Mercy appears in the Bible as it relates to forgiveness and withholding punishment but can also be defined as showing compassion, especially to an offender.

> *"You were taught, with regarding to your former way of life, to put off your old self, which is being corrupted by its deceitful desires; to be made new in the attitude of your minds."*
>
> Ephesians 4:22-23 (NIV)

Knowing these words is important. More important is putting these words to work for your relationship with yourself and others.

Extend grace because you understand that your partner is an imperfect human being. Extend grace because our Father never withholds grace from you. Inevitably, your partner will do things that will hurt you and will say things out of anger. Your partner will love you from a broken place but in their mind and heart, they feel that they are doing the best they can. Understanding and seeing your partner as someone worth being patient with and fighting for is important. Extending grace is challenging, but the effort is worth it.

Many of us are so hard on others, but when we make a mistake, we want them to forgive us easily. When we love the way God loves, our look on forgiveness dramatically changes. No matter what we do or how we mess up in life, God extends His grace and mercy upon us, and that is what we must learn to do with our partners. Grace has changed my outlook on my relationships because it allows me to be more understanding of my partner and the situation at hand. It has helped me to have more patience with my partner. I understand that in moments or circumstances, my partner could express herself from a place of pain or brokenness. Even though I may have caused that pain, I need to understand the importance of handling that moment. So, amid a difficult conversation with her, I need to understand her mental and emotional space.

Isn't it interesting how we respond in certain moments with certain people? We tend to give our children grace when they do something wrong. We may say they are young or didn't know any better, but why don't we do the same for adults? It's not to make an excuse for them but an attempt to be more understanding. When we work to provide for our families, we show grace toward people daily. In those moments, whether intentional or not, we won't do anything to jeopardize our money. By any means, we will act accordingly because we prioritize our responsibilities. We should do the same for our partner and relationship. You never know what you can teach a person by what you show them, and that's powerful.

Often, we give advice, encouraging others to be forgiving.

How can I tell you to forgive, be gracious, and be kind, but I'm not willing to do the same?

How can I ask something from someone or want the relationship to improve if I'm unwilling to show them?

We don't ask ourselves those questions.

We continue to do the same things repeatedly and wonder why our relationships don't improve or why growth as a couple is not happening. Well, the answer has to do with our mentality.

First, let's start with the fact that if your relationship is not improving or growth as a couple is not happening, there's a big probability that you are not growing individually nor putting in the necessary work to evolve and be what we ask of those in our lives. Then, add your expectations to that equation. We treat people with the "what have you done for me lately" mentality, and that's not good for the spirit. We should naturally live a life of love, peace, and understanding (Eph 4:22-32). I know grace isn't easy or favorable, but when you move with those principles, you start seeing blessings in all areas of your life, especially in your relationships.

## Chapter Nine

# SERVICE

*"Submit to one another out of reverence for Christ. Wives, submit yourselves to your own husbands as you do to the Lord. For the husband is the head of the wife as Christ is the head of the church, his body, of which he is the Savior. Now as the church submits to Christ, so also wives should submit to their husbands in everything. Husbands, love your wives, just as Christ loved the church and gave himself up for her to make her holy, cleansing her by the washing with water through the word, and to present her to himself as a radiant church, without stain or wrinkle or any other blemish, but holy and blameless. In this same way, husbands ought to love their wives*

*as their own bodies. He who loves his wife loves himself. After all, no one ever hated their own body, but they feed and care for their body, just as Christ does the church—for we are members of his body. 'For this reason a man will leave his father and mother and be united to his wife, and the two will become one flesh.' This is a profound mystery—but I am talking about Christ and the church. However, each one of you also must love his wife as he loves himself, and the wife must respect her husband."*

Ephesians 5:21-33 (NIV)

H AVE YOU EVER SAT BACK and considered different ways to serve your partner?

Some people may turn their noses up at that question because they read "serve" and immediately think of being a prisoner of service to someone else. However, service is vital to relationships. Genuine service aids in making your partner feel special, supported, and considered, but there's a formula to servitude: Serve God first, then serve your partner.

Take a moment to figure out how to be there for your partner and bring happiness to them.

How can you provide for them? (Note: This question goes far beyond the monetary sense).

How can you make them feel comfortable and safe?

How can you ease their mental, physical, or emotional load?

Those are some questions you should think about when it comes to your partner. You should do this consistently, not just on holidays or random occasions.

Unfortunately, we are too selfish these days. Everything is about me, myself, and I. We don't do for our partner, nor go above and beyond for our partner. After a while, we don't appreciate our partners the same way. We get comfortable; in a sense, we become accustomed to this pattern. That's a harsh truth many don't accept.

You hear people say all the time, "What can they do for me?"

Women usually refer to what men can do financially. That could mean paying their bills, buying things they like, or taking them on trips. For men, on the other hand, most of the time, it's sexual or what he desires. How many men would rub their woman's feet or do something special for them that has nothing to do with themselves? You are solely doing it for them because you care for them, removing yourself from the equation. Many people are in relationships because they're trying to get something out of it. The mentality is "If I'm nice, then I'll get this, or they will do that," instead of serving somebody because you love and care for them; our love is manipulative. We got away from the concept of putting our partners first, which is something we should automatically do for each other.

Prioritizing your partner does not mean neglecting your children or responsibilities. You can make your partner feel special daily by making small and consistent gestures. Go for walks, take rides, cook for them, wash the dishes, be present during a conversation, and hold them at night. Those are a few intentional acts to serve your partner and make them feel special. Ask them what they need. Do an act without them having to ask. Take time daily to display your love for them. People want to feel special every day, even with the smallest gesture.

Service removes pride and ego. When pride and ego enter the equation, people stop communicating with one another. When putting your partner first, elect to hear from them. Listen to hear, not to speak. When you put them first, you show how much you value the relationship. That does not mean you have to agree with the person. Many people argue because they want to be right, and that's why conflict lingers. They only focus on how they feel while neglecting the other person. A lot of relationships go down the drain because of that.

*"The real love we're seeking isn't a fairytale; it's the ability to actually be ourselves. What we want is to be seen, heard, and appreciated for who we are rather than molded into who someone wants us to be."*

Unknown

We talk about how we love our partners and want to connect with them, but our words must constantly match our actions. People tend to dive into relationships for all the wrong reasons. If you want a true relationship and partner, you will operate in a healthier manner. How you think, speak, and act within the relationship will be geared toward a healthy future. You should look at your partner as someone you want to have a solid foundation with. No obstacle is too tough to handle together. You both are confident, knowing you are going in the same direction together. You know someone is on your team; you're not against each other. Whatever you do as a couple, however you do it, you will be together. That's what a team is all about. Nothing feels better than clearly understanding where you are with your partner. That understanding comes from service and staying the course.

Speak often.

Listen often.

Give grace, be kind, and make your partner feel special and on top of the world.

Do those acts consistently.

> "Compromise is not about losing. It is about deciding that the other person has just as much right to be happy with the end result as you do."
>
> Donna Martini

Meeting each other in the middle is vital. Learning to compromise with your partner more often is essential to a healthy relationship. Have you ever watched how relationships play out among your peers or on social media? It's hard determining who to believe when people are arguing and dragging each other through the mud. If there were a compromise, you would move differently, even amid conflict, and moving differently starts with communication. If there were a change in how thoughts are communicated, there would be an easier path to resolution. Love is so powerful, and it conquers all. That display of love will have you apologizing for things you shouldn't be sorry for because that type of love humbles you. That type of love will have you wanting to listen and understand versus being hell-bent on winning. That type of love will have you wanting things to be calm and cool so a real conversation can be had at the right time. There's always a place, time, and way to address your concerns or issues. Doing it with love shows your partner that you value the relationship and, most importantly, that you value them.

Looking back at my career, I think of the teams I've been on and my different roles. I've played for teams that have been more successful than others, but I had a role with each of those teams. Roles play a major part in every team, and knowing your role is the key to success. Each player should know their role and perform the duties that come with it daily (humility and service). Coming with the right mindset consistently and not getting sidetracked is fundamental to achieving the big goal. Doesn't everyone want to win a championship? Well, in relationships, the "team" should have a goal of longevity, working together, doing their part, and performing their respective duties to have a healthy, long-lasting relationship. Within any team, the qualities and characteristics should be geared toward building a winning culture. That foundation will breed success if consistency plays a continual factor. Having the right mindset, eliminating pride and egos, and remembering accountability is extremely important. Do not be that teammate that wants to blame everyone else during a season or relationship. Be the responsible teammate that does their part. Because this is a team, we acknowledge that a relationship is not a competition between one another. Stop the comparison game. Your partner, along with your relationship, is special within itself and should be valued as such.

> *"Instagram has ruined a whole generation's expectations of relationships, work, and everything in between. It has made 'perfect' look normal, so now 'good' has become disposable."*
>
> Steven Bartlett

It's easy to mask who you are with social media. You can pretend that you have it all together. You can also make it seem like you are living a perfect life despite what's really going on. You compare yourself and other areas in your life, trying to compete with your timeline. Your perception can also get in the way of how you function relationally. Social media has made it acceptable to switch up when you are unhappy with the person you say you love. It's deemed normal or commonplace to disrespect someone you claim you want to be with versus building healthy communication skills offline. Social media also has couples competing with each other, but not in a healthy way. Women don't need men because they can do what men do, and men feel like they can't be with a successful woman because of insecurities. Social media has also turned relationships into finding business partners. So much of why couples are together is because of what someone can do for them. Materialism has taken over. Most of the time, relationships aren't about love. They're for show and status. Love should be at the very core and foundation of a relationship.

Love is when you love someone for who they are and don't try to change them. We don't operate in love enough. In many cases, someone is trying to change something about their partner in some way, shape, or form. We must get to a point where we understand that if someone wants to change, they will. I want to live my life and love the way the Heavenly Father and Mother speak about in 1 Corinthians 13:4-7. I don't base my love on what someone does for me or how they make me feel. Service is important, but giving and receiving acts of love should come from the heart, not as a measure of whether I'll stay or go. I love because of who I am and what I want to give my partner. I love because I am an example of love and how love continues to show up for me from the creator. Relationships do not have to be complicated, especially if we are in them for the right reasons.

Everyone wants to be treated like royalty, which is a great expectation because we are special in our own right. Everyone wants the love and respect they envision. People want a partner who will go above and beyond for their needs. Whether people realize it or not, they expect service. Yet, how many are willing to give what they expect? Who is willing to show up for their partner when they feel they aren't showing up for you? How many of us love from a conditional cup? Is that fair? No! We have to get out of our selfish ways. We must learn to appreciate our partners, forgive, and be gracious and merciful.

You should love your partner for who they are and not through the lens you want to see. Show your love through your actions and not just with your words. Love your partner correctly. Be intentional with every thought and action. Make the most out of each moment. Understand the power of being truly present with your partner. Learn to be the bigger person during trying times. Apologize first, even if there are times in which you aren't the offender. If you love your partner the way you say you do, make sure you do the personal work for yourself. Make sure you are the best version of yourself to give your partner everything and then some. Make sure to focus on your part in the success of the relationship you desire to have. Understand there will be good and bad days.

Know that you have the power to create whatever environment you desire in your relationship. Make sure to express yourself clearly in matters that are important to you. Don't apologize for how you feel but make sure you communicate as healthily as possible. Serve your partner and put them first. Fight for them daily. Make sure you reassure them without asking so they know you are where they want to be. Take time at least once a day to tell them that you are thankful for them and why. The goal is healthiness across the board, to have a mentally, emotionally, spiritually, financially, and physically healthy and happy relationship. That's what we should desire and be willing to do by any means necessary.

# Closing

I'VE ALWAYS HAD A VISION where men and women worked on themselves and put in the time and effort to become healthy versions of themselves. That type of effort sets a foundation that allows people to attract healthy relationships – personally and professionally. This foundation allows you to be more intentional and attract what is meant for you, especially relationships that serve you and your life's purpose.

A healthier you is accountable for your actions.

A healthier you is responsible for the decisions you make and uses each lesson as a tool to help you evolve.

When you are in a healthier place in life, you understand your red flags, how to enforce boundaries, and how to express yourself. You understand that you can love someone and fight for them without losing yourself, and by fighting, I'm referring to effort – not toxic communication and other negative behaviors.

Small conversations and eye contact matter and being present at the moment is necessary for building something special with your partner.

Care for your partner in such a way that you want to learn every side of them and grow with them. Be willing to love them where they are and not try to change them into who you want them to be. Encourage their growth, yes, but avoid the act of changing them into what you deem suitable. Love someone for them and not what they can do for you.

I understand many things make for a healthy relationship, but having love as the foundation is essential. Communication, kindness, respect, loyalty, honesty, and grace are a few things on the list of many that are essential to a strong relationship, but true love will let you know your partner is the one you will grow old with until God calls you home.

# About the Author

Josh "JP" Powell was born in Charleston, SC and raised in College Park, GA. His southern charm and a sense of service has groomed him for greatness. Having earned a full scholarship to ACC contender North Carolina State University, Josh decided to leave college after only two years to pursue a professional basketball career.

This choice served him well, because for more than two decades, JP has been making an impact on the court. During his basketball tenure, he became a 2x NBA champion with the Los Angeles Lakers, a Euroleague champion with Olympiacos, and he's still in the game as the current co-captain for the BIG3 Killer 3's.

As a regional representative for the NBPA in the player programming department, JP uses his insider knowledge of sports, global view from extensive travels, broad perspective on relationships, entertainment, lifestyle and philanthropy to help people of all ages grow to be better versions of themselves.

JP has been transparent and vocal about his love for his children and the trials of his unique fatherhood journey, as he has children by multiple women. This reality has made him a passionate advocate for fathers' rights. Possessing a strong affinity for relationship talk, JP has a distinct ability to change the narrative on the complexities of not only romantic relationships, but ALL relationships.

Navigating challenging dynamics in his own life allows JP to appreciate first-hand the importance of prioritizing wellness and life balance. He founded the 21 Reasons To Give Foundation to assist impoverished areas and restore those who are suffering. JP is committed to a life of growth and service in which he hopes to touch all in his sphere of influence.

JP is co-creator of the Relationships Matter podcast, and author of the new book, *"What I Wish I Knew: The Wisdom Gained From Relationships, Love, and Lust."* In his book, JP speaks to the work, vulnerability, acceptance and many discomforting things that it takes to create true love— a rare creation that JP says starts with giving and receiving every day.

This athlete, author, activist and love advocate says "We need to get back to loving the way that God intended for us to love and not the way that human beings have translated, tarnished or turned 'love' for ourselves." He believes that what we tend to do as humans has failed us, but if we move and operate the way the Creator wants us to, we can build better homes with stronger foundations, better communities and the list goes on. Doing relationships better is worth it!

Josh's motto is "If it's worth it, fight for it."